DOGS JUST KNOW

Written by M.H. Clark | Illustrated by Emily Taylor

Dogs know that the day is worth waking for...
whatever it may bring.

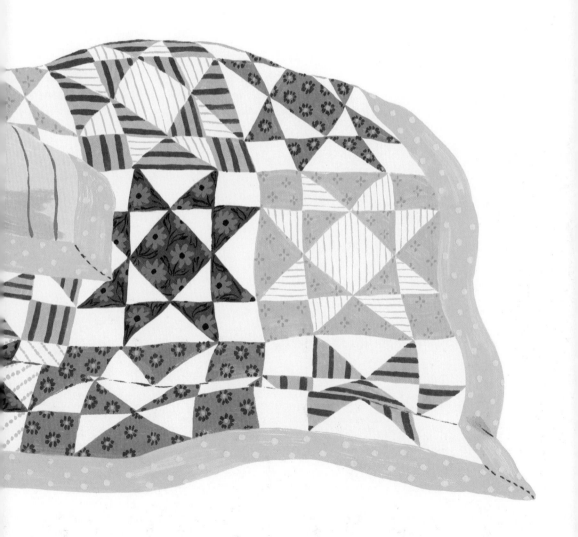

Dogs cherish what is here because it is good.
Dogs know there are no little things.

*Dogs know that it's okay to like what you like
and love what you love.*

Dogs don't judge.

*Dogs know that being true to yourself
is the best way to be.*

Dogs know that you should always
ask for what you want.
(And if it doesn't work at first, keep asking.)

Dogs know that you should
expect nice things to happen to you.
(Because they often do.)

*Dogs know that no matter how great we are,
we're even greater together.*

Dogs know we are here for each other.
And that love changes us for the better.

Dogs know that being unique is a marvelous thing.

Dogs know that we deserve a little treat.
Every day. Just for being.

Dogs know that the best things are worth taking a risk.
And that sometimes, getting into trouble is worth it.

Dogs know that play is important.
And silliness is good.

Dogs don't take themselves too seriously.
(And they know that no one should.)

Dogs know the best moment
is the moment we are in.

And that there is so much joy in living our favorite
routines again and again and again.

Dogs know that almost everything can be fixed with a kiss.

(Dogs even suspect this is why they exist.)

Dogs know that love needs no words...
especially when we understand each other.

Dogs know that enthusiasm is always appropriate.
And that when we care about people, we have to show it.

Dogs just know what matters most.
And then, they teach us too.

Dogs change us for the better,
with everything they do.

COMPENDIUM.
live inspired

Written by: M.H. Clark

Illustrated by: Emily Taylor

Edited by: Bailey Vega

Art Directed by: Chelsea Bianchini

ISBN: 978-1-957891-28-6

1st printing. Printed in China with soy inks on FSC®-Mix certified paper.

Create meaningful moments with gifts that inspire.

CONNECT WITH US
live-inspired.com | sayhello@compendiuminc.com

     @compendiumliveinspired
#compendiumliveinspired